Did you know that there are many ways to say grandpa in Chinese? It can vary by region or area your family is from. Here are some common ways to address grandpa.

Maternal side

外祖父 "ngoi6 zou2 fu6"
外公 "ngoi6 gung1"
阿公 "aa3 gung1"
公公 "gung4 gung1"

Paternal side

祖父 "zou2 fu6"
爺爺 "je4 je2"

Mina uses 公公 (gung4 gung1) to address her grandpa, but feel free to interchange it to whichever way your child addresses his/her grandpa.

For my Dad, Mina's "gong gong"

For a FREE audio reading and other bilingual books visit:
www.minalearnschinese.com

Follow us

Minalearnschinese

ISBN: 978-1-953281-60-9
Also available in Traditional and Simplified Chinese Editions!
Copyright © 2022   All rights reserved.

Our pup, Musubi

Translations by
Dr. Chaak-Ming Lau, Dr. Lee Dennig,
Ella Tam and Cantonese Mommy
www.CantoneseMommy.com

mai5 naa4: gung4 gung1, ngo5 jau5 go3 zyu2 ji3!

米娜：公公，我有個主意！

Mina: Grandpa, I have an idea!

mai5 naa4: ngo5 waak6 bei2 nei5 tai2, hou2 m4 hou2 aa3?

米娜：我畫畀你睇，好唔好呀？

Mina: I will draw it for you to see okay?

gung4 gung1: hou2 aa3, mai5 naa4!

公公：好呀，米娜！

Grandpa: Sure, Mina!

mai5 naa4: nei5 tai2 ngo5 waak6 zo2 mat1 je5!

米娜：你睇我畫咗乜嘢！

Mina: Look at what I drew!

gung4 gung1: aa1, ngo5 zi1 dou6! jat1 ding6 hai6 siu2 mai5 gaan1 gau2 uk1!

公公：啊，我知道！一定係小米間狗屋！

Grandpa: Ah, I know! This must be Musubi's dog house!

mai5 naa4: Gung4 gung1, nei5 zung1 m4 zung1 ji3 ngo5 waak6 ge3 fan2 hung4 sik1 uk1 deng2 aa3?

米娜：公公，你鍾唔鍾意我畫嘅粉紅色屋頂呀？

Mina: Grandpa, do you like the pink roof that I drew?

Gung4 gung1: zung1 ji3 aa3!

公公：鍾意呀！

Grandpa: I do like it!

mai5 naa4: siu2 mai5 zung1 ji3 hung4 sik1 ge3 faa1.

米娜：小米鍾意紅色嘅花。

Mina: Musubi likes red flowers.

gung4 gung1: waak6 dak1 hou2 leng3 aa3, mai5 naa4!

公公：畫得好靚呀，米娜！

Grandpa: So beautifully drawn, Mina!

mai5 naa4: gung4 gung1, nei5 ho2 m4 ho2 ji5 hei2 ni1 gaan1 gau2 uk1 ceot1 lai4 aa3?

米娜：公公，你可唔可以起呢間狗屋出嚟呀？

Mina: Grandpa, can you build this dog house?

gung4 gung1: gang2 hai6 ho2 ji5 laa1, daan6 hai6 ngo5 seoi1 jiu3 jat1 go3 siu2 bong1 sau2.

公公：梗係可以喇，但係我需要一個小幫手。

Grandpa: Of course I can, but I'll need an assistant.

gung4 gung1: nei5 wui2 m4 wui2 bong1 ngo5 aa3?

公公：你會唔會幫我呀？

Grandpa: Would you be willing to help me?

mai5 naa4: ngo5 gang2 hai6 wui5 laa1!

米娜：我梗係會啦！

Mina: Yes, I'd love to!

mai5 naa4: gung4 gung1, ngo5 dei6 jing1 goi1 zou6 mat1 je5 sin1 aa3?

米娜：公公，我哋應該做乜嘢先呀？

Mina: Grandpa, what should we do first?

gung4 gung1: ngo5 dei6 jat1 cai4 heoi3 ce1 fong4 wan2 gung1 geoi6 tung4 coi4 liu2 sin1 laa1!

公公：我哋一齊去車房搵工具同材料先啦！

Grandpa: Let's first go to the garage to find tools and materials!

公公: _{gung4 gung1:} _{ngo5 dei6 seoi1 jiu3 gei2 faai3 muk6 baan2,} _{jat1 go3 ceoi4 zai2 tung4 jat1 di1}
我哋需要幾塊木板，一個鎚仔同一啲

_{ding1.} _{gau2 uk1 jing1 goi1 hei2 hai2 bin1 dou6 aa3?}
釘。狗屋應該起喺邊度呀？

Grandpa: We'll need a few wood planks, a hammer, and some nails. Where should we build the dog house?

mai5 naa4: ngo5 gok3 dak1 hau6 jyun2 po1 daai6 syu6 haa6 min6 hai6 go3 hou2 dei6 fong1.

米娜：我覺得後院棵大樹下面係個好地方。

Mina: I think under the big tree in the backyard is a good spot.

公公: gung4 gung1: ceoi4 zai2 hai2 bin1 dou6 ne1?
鎚仔喺邊度呢?
Grandpa: Where's the hammer?

米娜: mai5 naa4: hai2 ni1 dou6, gung4 gung1!
喺呢度，公公！
Mina: It's over here, Grandpa!

公公: gung4 gung1: m4 goi1 saai3! nei5 zan1 hai6 go3 hou2 bong1 sau2!
唔該晒! 你真係個好幫手！
Grandpa: Thank you! You're such a great helper!

gung4 gung1: hei2 hou2 laa3!　　nei5 gok3 dak1 dim2 aa3?

公公：起好喇！你覺得點呀？

Grandpa: All done! What do you think?

mai5 naa4: tung4 ngo5 waak6 ge3　m4　jat1 joeng6.

米娜：同我畫嘅唔一樣。

Mina: It's not exactly like my drawing.

gung4 gung1: gong2 dak1 ngaam1! gam2 siu2 zo2 mat1 je5 ne1?

公公：講得啱！咁少咗乜嘢呢？

Grandpa: You're right! What's it missing?

mai5 naa4: gung4 gung1, ngo5 zi1 laa3!

米娜：公公，我知喇！

siu2 zo2 di1 ngaan4 sik1.

少咗啲顏色。

Mina: Grandpa, I know!
It's missing color!

公公: gung4 gung1: ngo5 dei6 jau5 zi2 sik1, laam4 sik1, fan2 hung4 sik1 tung4 maai4 wong4 sik1 ge3 jau4 cat1. gaan2 me1 ngaan4 sik1 hou2 ne1?

公公:我哋有紫色，藍色，粉紅色同埋黃色嘅油漆。揀咩顏色好呢？

Grandpa: We have purple, blue, pink, and yellow paint. Which colors should we use?

mai5 naa4: ngo5 soeng2 jau4 ngo5 zeoi3 zung1 ji3 ge3 loeng5 zung2 ngaan4 sik1

米娜：我想髹我最鍾意嘅兩種顏色，

wong4 sik1 tung4 fan2 hung4 sik1!

黃色同粉紅色！

Mina: I'd like to paint it with my two favorite colors, yellow and pink!

mai5 naa4: gung4 gung1, ngo5 jau4 jyun4 laa3!

米娜：公公，我髹完喇！

Mina: Grandpa, I'm done painting!

gung4 gung1: taai3 hou2 laa3! ngo5 dei6 seoi1 jiu3 dang2 di1 jau4 cat1 bin3 gon1.

公公：太好喇！我哋需要等啲油漆變乾。

Grandpa: It's terrific! We need to wait for the paint to dry.

gung4 gung1: ji4 gaa1 jau1 sik1 jat1 zan6,
公公：而家休息一陣，

hou2 m4 hou2 aa3?
好唔好呀？

Grandpa: How about we take a break?

gung4 gung1: ngo5 dei6 lai4 je5 caan1 laa1!

公公：我哋嚟野餐啦！

Grandpa: Let's have a picnic!

mai5 naa4: waa3 gung4 gung1! ngo5 zeoi3 zung1 ji3 ge3 je5 sik6!

米娜：嘩公公！我最鍾意嘅嘢食！

saam1 man4 zi6, gwo2 zap1 tung4 saang1 gwo2!

三文治，果汁同生果！

Mina: Wow, Grandpa! My favorites! Sandwiches, juice, and fruit!

mai5 naa4: siu2 mai5 tai2 lai4 dou1 soeng2 sik6 di1 siu2 sik6 wo3.

米娜：小米睇嚟都想食啲小食喎。

lai4 sik6 laa1, siu2 mai5!

嚟食啦，小米！

Mina: It looks like Musubi wants a snack too. Come and eat, Musubi!

gung4 gung1: jau4 cat1 gon1 zo2 laa3. tai2 haa5 siu2 mai5
公公：油漆乾咗喇。睇下小米

zung1 m4 zung1 ji3 gaan1 uk1.
鍾唔鍾意間屋。

Grandpa: The paint is dry. Time to see if Musubi likes her new house.

mai5 naa4: ngo5 gok3 dak1 keoi5 hou2 zung1 ji3!
米娜：我覺得佢好鍾意！

Mina: I think she likes it!

mai5 naa4: do1 ze6 gung4 gung1 pui4 ngo5!

米娜：多謝公公陪我！

ngo5 gam1 jat6 hou2 hoi1 sam1 aa3!

我今日好開心呀！

ngo5 oi3 nei5!

我愛你！

Mina: Thank you, Grandpa for hanging out with me!
I'm so happy today! I love you!

gung4 gung1: ngo5 dou1 hou2 oi3 nei5!

公公：我都好愛你！

Grandpa: I love you too!

Made in the USA
Las Vegas, NV
12 October 2023